DOMINOES

The Tempest

STARTER LEVEL 250 HEADWORDS

OXFORD
UNIVERSITY PRESS

Great Clarendon Street, Oxford OX2 6DP

Oxford University Press is a department of the University of Oxford.
It furthers the University's objective of excellence in research, scholarship, and education by publishing worldwide in

Oxford New York

Auckland Cape Town Dar es Salaam Hong Kong Karachi Kuala Lumpur Madrid Melbourne Mexico City Nairobi New Delhi Shanghai Taipei Toronto

With offices in

Argentina Austria Brazil Chile Czech Republic France Greece Guatemala Hungary Italy Japan Poland Portugal Singapore South Korea Switzerland Thailand Turkey Ukraine Vietnam

First published in Dominoes 2004

2022

25

ISBN: 978 0 19 424707 8 Book
ISBN: 978 0 19 463931 6 Book and Audio Pack

Printed in China

This book is printed on paper from certified and well-managed sources.

ACKNOWLEDGEMENTS

Illustrations by: Andy Parker

The publisher would like to thank the following for permission to reproduce photographs: OUP ppiv (Lightening bolts/Warren Faidley/Corbis), 41 (Cook Islands/Photodisc).

For my mother Clarissa Gloria Spencer (1930–1997) who gave me my love of Shakespeare and of the theatre

Bill Bowler

DOMINOES

Series Editors: Bill Bowler and Sue Parminter

The Tempest

William Shakespeare

Text adaptation by Bill Bowler

Illustrated by Andy Parker

William Shakespeare (1564–1616) was born and grew up in Stratford-upon-Avon. At the age of twenty-five, he left his wife and children in Stratford, moved to London, and started working as an actor and writer at the Globe Theatre. Shakespeare wrote more than thirty plays, and some fine poetry too. He wrote *The Tempest* in 1611, and it is his only play with an original story – usually Shakespeare retold other people's stories. Shakespeare's plays are still famous all over the world today, and for many people he is the greatest writer in English.

OXFORD
UNIVERSITY PRESS

ACTIVITIES

BEFORE READING

1 Here are some of the people in the story *The Tempest*. Look at the pictures and answer the questions.

1 ALONSO

2 ANTONIO

3 FERDINAND

4 MIRANDA

5 PROSPERO

6 SEBASTIAN

a Who is Prospero's brother? ☐

b Who is Ferdinand's father? ☐

c Who is Alonso's brother? ☐

d Who is Miranda's father? ☐

e Who is Miranda's lover? ☐

f Who are Antonio's friends? ☐☐

2 'Tempest' is an old word from Shakespeare's time for 'storm'. Tick the boxes to complete this sentence.

☐ Antonio
☐ Ferdinand
☐ Prospero

starts the tempest because he is

☐ afraid.
☐ angry.
☐ in love.

duke the most important man in a big old town

wife a woman living with a man

look after to do things for someone or something that needs help

magic something that makes things happen in a way that you don't understand

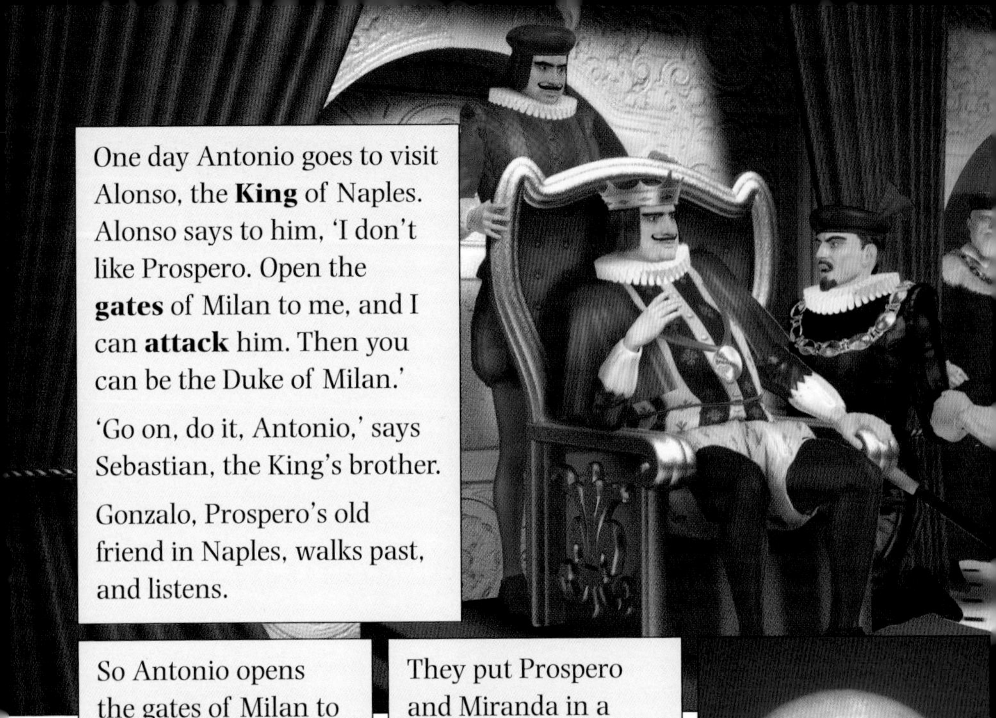

One day Antonio goes to visit Alonso, the **King** of Naples. Alonso says to him, 'I don't like Prospero. Open the **gates** of Milan to me, and I can **attack** him. Then you can be the Duke of Milan.'

'Go on, do it, Antonio,' says Sebastian, the King's brother.

Gonzalo, Prospero's old friend in Naples, walks past, and listens.

So Antonio opens the gates of Milan to King Alonso.

They put Prospero and Miranda in a little **boat** . . .

. . . and leave them far out at sea.

king the most important man in a country, or an old town

gate the big door into a town

attack to start hitting someone suddenly

boat you go across the water in this

In the boat Prospero finds a **letter** from Gonzalo:

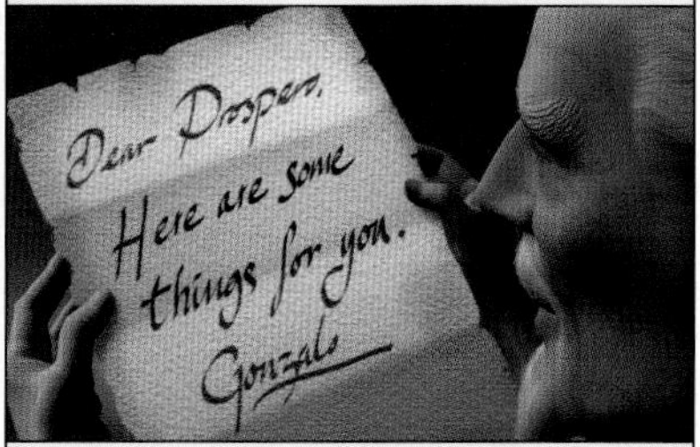

And Prospero finds things to eat, drink, and wear, and his magic book, too.
'Good old Gonzalo! What a true friend!' he thinks.

The little boat moves across the sea to a magic **island**.

The **monster** Caliban is king of the island. His mother is dead, and he has no friends.

Different magic **spirits** live on the island, too. They don't like Caliban.

letter you write this to tell something to someone

island a country in the sea

monster a person or animal that is very bad to look at

spirit a magic person without a body

show to help someone to see something

ship a big boat

ACTIVITIES

READING CHECK

Choose the correct pictures.

a ... lives in Milan with his wife and daughter.

ANTONIO

GONZALO

PROSPERO

b Alonso, the King of Naples, doesn't like ...

GONZALO

PROSPERO

SEBASTIAN

c Alonso and Antonio leave ... far out at sea in a boat.

MIRANDA AND PROSPERO

GONZALO AND SEBASTIAN

SEBASTIAN AND PROSPERO

d ... is Prospero's true friend.

ANTONIO

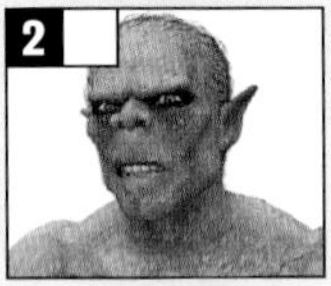

CALIBAN

GONZALO

e ... teaches Caliban to speak.

ARIEL

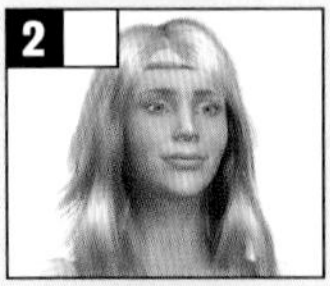

MIRANDA

PROSPERO

f Prospero sees ... on a ship near his island.

ARIEL AND CALIBAN

ANTONIO AND ALONSO

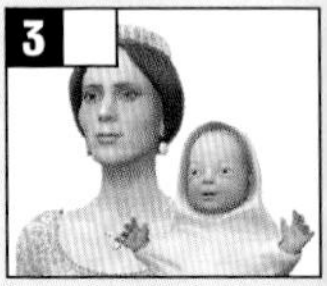

HIS WIFE AND BABY MIRANDA

WORD WORK

These words don't match the pictures. Correct them.

a ~~king~~ .....ship......

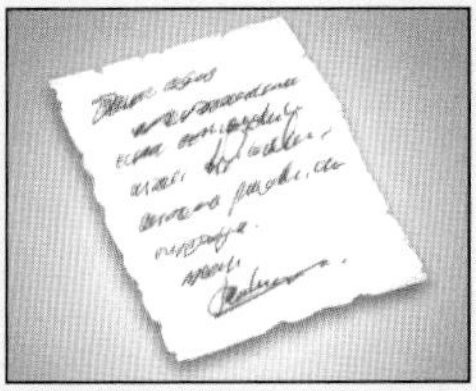

b island ....

c ship ....

d letter ....

e gates ....

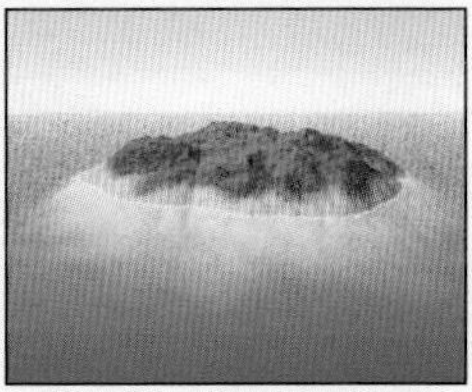

f boat ....

Find words from Chapter 1 to complete the sentences.

a Prospero's wife dies when Miranda is very young.

b Prospero is the true d _ _ _ of Milan.

c Antonio looks a_ _ _ _ Milan when Prospero is studying.

d Antonio helps Alonso to a_ _ _ _ _ Milan.

e Prospero and Miranda arrive on a m_ _ _ _ island.

f Ariel is a s_ _ _ _ _ on the island.

g Caliban is a m_ _ _ _ _ _.

h Caliban s_ _ _ _ Prospero everything on the island.

GUESS WHAT

What does Prospero say to Ariel in the next chapter? Tick one box.

a ☐ 'Kill Antonio and Alonso for me!'

b ☐ 'Take Miranda and me to the ship.'

c ☐ 'Attack the ship with a tempest.'

d ☐ 'Take Caliban to the ship.'

2 The Tempest

'There is a ship near my island,' Prospero tells Ariel. 'Make a magic **storm** and attack the ship.'

'The men on the ship must not die,' says Prospero. 'They must **land** on the island. The King's son, Ferdinand, must land **alone**.'

So Ariel goes to the ship, and makes a **tempest** with **wind** and rain.

storm a lot of rain and very bad weather

land to arrive somewhere from a ship

alone with nobody

tempest an old word for 'storm'

wind fast moving air

God an important being who never dies and who decides what happens in the world

captain the most important sailor on a ship

jump to move suddenly from one place to a different place

swim to go through the water moving your arms and legs

alive not dead

river water that moves through the country in a long line

part some, but not all, of something

naster you call the person that you vork for this

vood the hard part of a tree

ire this is red and hot, and it burns

READING CHECK

Match the pictures with the sentences.

a . . . tells Ariel, 'Attack the ship.'

b . . . makes a storm over the ship.

c . . . is the first to leave the ship.

d . . . says to Prospero, 'Stop the storm.'

e . . . tells Miranda, 'Don't be afraid.'

f . . . goes to sleep when Ariel is talking to Prospero.

g . . . goes to bring Ferdinand to Prospero.

WORD WORK

1 Find fifteen words from Chapter 2 in Prospero's book of magic.

A	C	H	D	S	N	F	M	M	A
O	C	A	P	T	A	I	N	A	J
S	G	L	U	O	E	R	R	S	S
S	W	I	M	R	B	E	F	T	I
S	I	V	U	M	P	F	I	E	D
O	N	E	I	R	I	V	E	R	S
W	D	W	L	F	A	R	M	M	A
P	U	W	A	I	J	U	M	P	J
A	L	O	N	E	K	D	I	X	Z
R	G	O	D	F	X	D	S	S	P
T	G	D	T	E	M	P	E	S	T

Match the words in Activity 1 with these sentences.

a Ariel makes a magic ...storm.... over Alonso's ship with a strong .... and lots of rain.

b .... is an old word for 'storm'.

c Ariel calls Prospero, '.................'.

d The .... of the ship cries for help.

e Alonso and Ferdinand ask .... for help.

f Ferdinand is the first to .... from the ship and .... away.

g Ariel puts Alonso's ship in one of the island's ....

h The men on the ship don't die; they are .... but sleeping.

i Ferdinand arrives on the island with nobody; he is ....

j Alonso, Sebastian, and Gonzalo .... in a different .... of the island.

k Caliban must get .... for Prospero's ....

GUESS WHAT

What happens in the next chapter? Tick two boxes.

a ☐ Ferdinand meets Miranda and loves her at once.

b ☐ Prospero is nice to Ferdinand.

c ☐ Prospero isn't nice to Ferdinand.

d ☐ Miranda doesn't like Ferdinand.

3 Prince Ferdinand

Ariel sings to **Prince** Ferdinand. 'Your father is dead!'

prince the son of a king

music singing or playing instruments

follow to go after something or somebody

plan when you get something ready before it happens

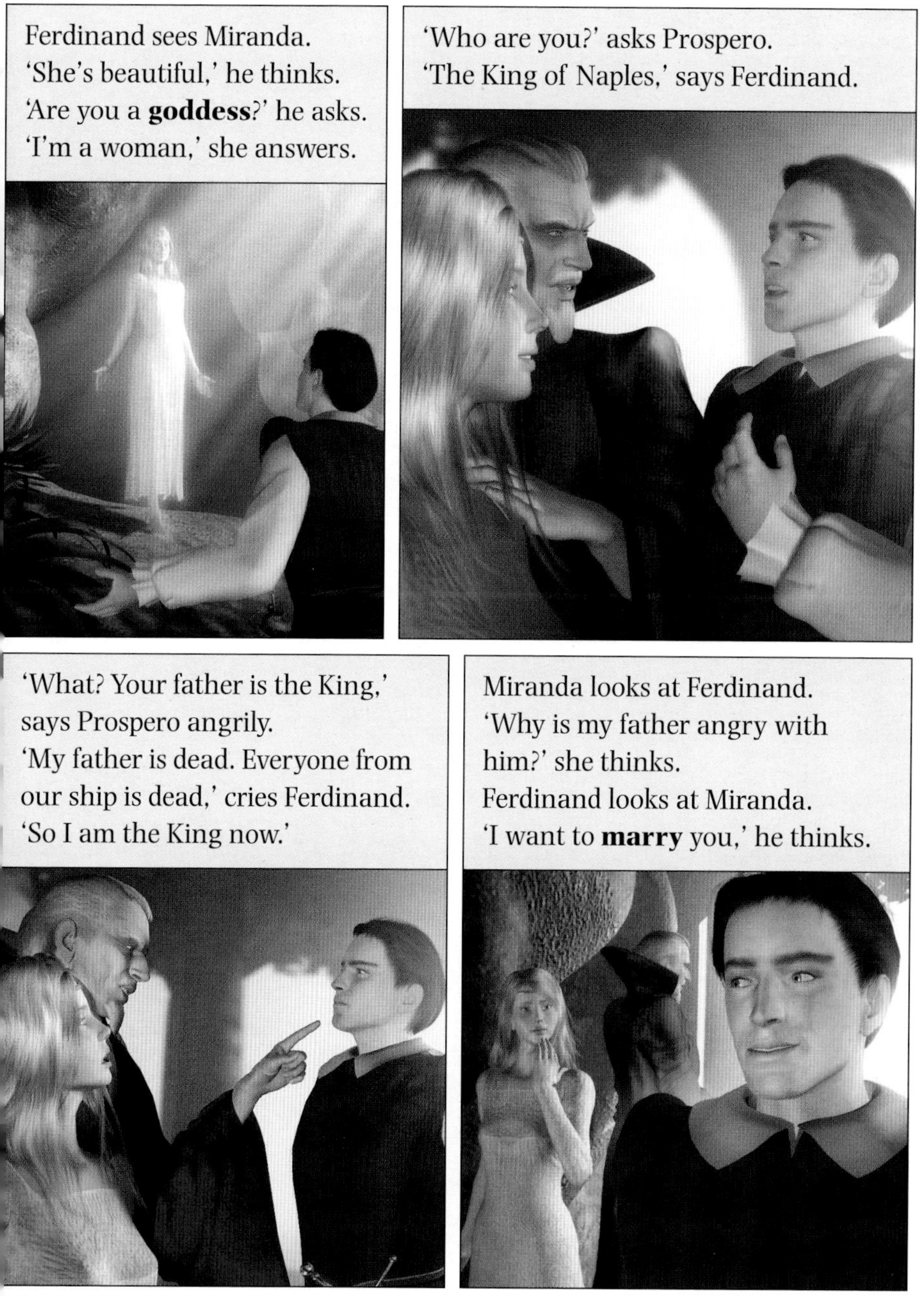

goddess a woman god

marry to make someone your wife or husband

difficult not easy

spy a person who tries to learn secret things

'My magic is stronger than your sword,' says Prospero. 'Now you are my prisoner!'
'I'm happy to be in prison here,' thinks Ferdinand, and he looks at Miranda, 'because now I can see more of *her*.'

'I don't understand,' says Miranda to the prince quietly. 'My father is usually nicer than this.'
'Ariel, come here. I have more work for you,' says Prospero.

chains long strings of metal; in these you cannot run away

prison a place where people must stay when they do something wrong

sword a long, sharp knife for fighting

READING CHECK

Match the two parts of the sentences.

a Ariel sings to . . .	**1** see Ariel.
b Ferdinand can't . . .	**2** Ferdinand a lot, too.
c Ariel brings . . .	**3** Ferdinand about his father.
d Ferdinand likes . . .	**4** Ferdinand when her father isn't looking.
e Miranda likes . . .	**5** angry with Ferdinand.
f Prospero is . . .	**6** understand her father.
g Miranda can't . . .	**7** Miranda a lot.
h Miranda talks nicely to . . .	**8** more work.
i Prospero gives Ariel . . .	**9** Ferdinand to Prospero.

WORD WORK

1 Find the words in the books to complete the sentences.

a Ferdinand says, 'Now my father is dead, I'm the King of Naples, not the Prince.'

b Lovers can't have everything easy all the time; d_ _ _ _ _ _ _ _ _ times are good for them.

c Ferdinand gets ready to fight and takes his s_ _ _ _ in his hand.

d Ferdinand can't leave Prospero's home. It's his p_ _ _ _ _ .

e Venus is the g _ _ _ _ _ _ of love.

ACTIVITIES

Correct the mistakes in these sentences.

a Ferdinand can hear Ariel's **magic** but can't see him. .....music.....

b Ferdinand **flowers** Ariel's music, and goes to Prospero. ....

c Prospero's **plane** is working. ....

d Ferdinand wants to **carry** Miranda. ....

e 'You are a **shy** !' says Prospero to Ferdinand. ....

f Prospero puts **trains** on Ferdinand. ....

GUESS WHAT

What happens in the next chapter? Write *Yes* or *No* for each picture.

a King Alonso finds Ferdinand. ....

b Ariel brings things to eat and drink for King Alonso. ....

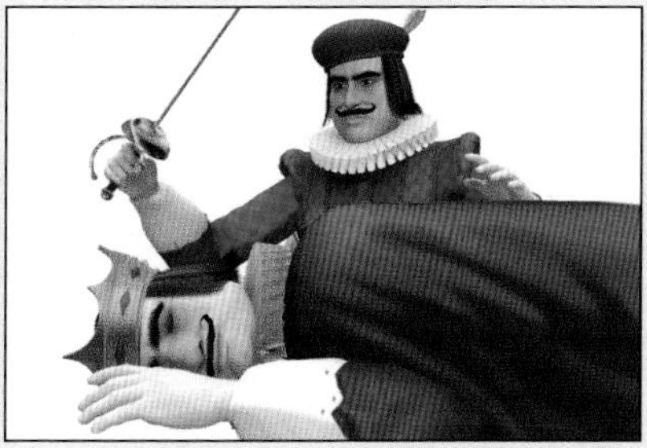

c Sebastian kills King Alonso when he is sleeping. ....

d Ariel attacks King Alonso. ....

4 The King & the Duke

King Alonso, Gonzalo, Antonio, and Sebastian are in a different part of the island.
'What a green island!' says Gonzalo.
'Very green!' laughs Antonio, and he and Sebastian look down at the yellow **ground** under their feet, and smile.

'Stop laughing,' says Alonso. 'My son is dead!' he cries.
'We don't know that,' says Gonzalo. 'Perhaps he's here on the island.'

Ariel comes to them. They can't see him, but they can hear his magic music. When Alonso and Gonzalo go to sleep Antonio says to Sebastian:
'Now Ferdinand is dead, you can be king when Alonso dies. So shall I kill him for you?'
'Yes!' says Sebastian. 'And let's kill Gonzalo, too. Then he can't talk.'

ground we walk on this

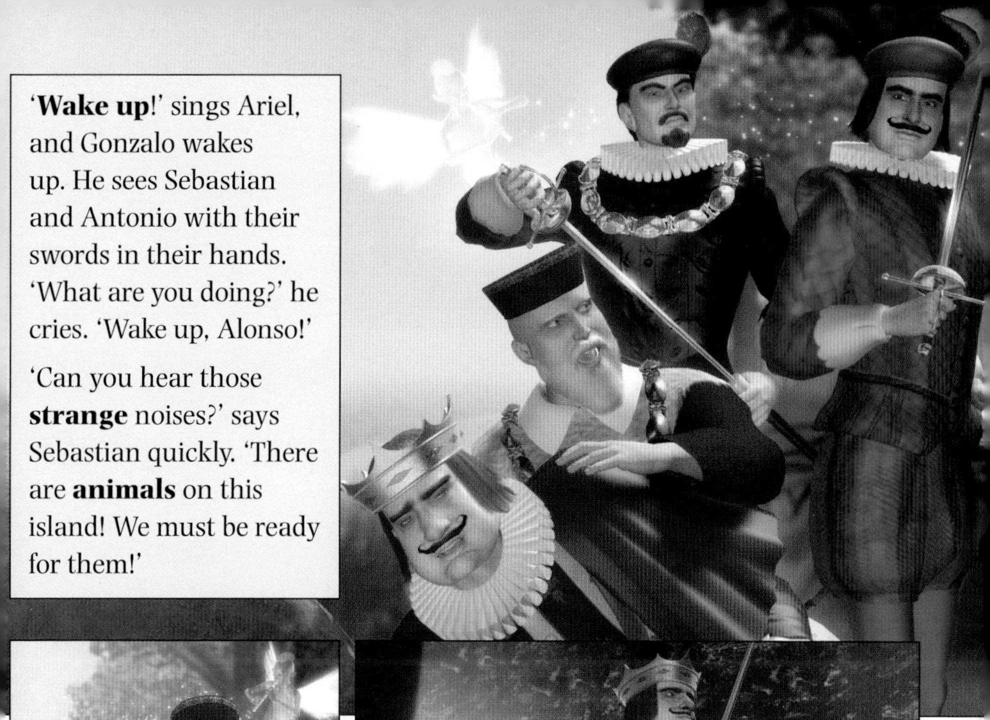

'**Wake up**!' sings Ariel, and Gonzalo wakes up. He sees Sebastian and Antonio with their swords in their hands. 'What are you doing?' he cries. 'Wake up, Alonso!'

'Can you hear those **strange** noises?' says Sebastian quickly. 'There are **animals** on this island! We must be ready for them!'

'I can hear *something*!' says Gonzalo. 'Let's all take out our swords.'

'I can't hear any noises,' says Alonso. 'Let's look for Ferdinand. I must find him – dead or alive.'

So Alonso, Gonzalo, Sebastian, and Antonio walk through the **forest**, and look for Ferdinand. Soon they feel tired and hungry.
'Let's kill them tonight,' says Antonio.
'All right,' says Sebastian.

wake up to stop sleeping

strange not usual

animal a living being that can think and move

forest a place with lots of trees

fool someone who cannot think well

pay to lose something because you do a bad thing to someone

crime killing someone, or taking something from someone

against not helping

READING CHECK

What do they say?

'Perhaps he's here on the island – alive.' **a** [2]

'You can be king when Alonso dies.' **b** [ ]

'Shall I kill Alonso for you?' **c** [ ]

'And I can kill Gonzalo for you.' **d** [ ]

'I must find him – dead or alive.' **e** [ ]

'You cannot attack us with swords!' **f** [ ]

'When you do bad things, bad things happen to you.' **g** [ ]

'Your son is dead!' **h** [ ]

'I want to die!' **i** [ ]

WORD WORK

Use the words from the magic table to complete the sentences on page 25.

a Antonio and Sebastian look at the yellow ...ground... under their feet, and laugh at Gonzalo with his talk of a 'green island'.

b Ariel sings, '.................. ....!' to Gonzalo when Antonio and Sebastian are coming to kill him and the King.

c Sebastian, Antonio, and Gonzalo can all hear .... noises on the magic island.

d Sebastian says, 'There are .... on this island!'

e Ariel calls Alonso, Sebastian, and Antonio, '..................' because they want to attack him.

f Ariel says to Alonso, 'You must .... for your past .... in Milan .... Prospero!'

g In the end Alonso runs away into the ....

GUESS WHAT

What happens in the next chapter? Tick the boxes.

a Ferdinand . . .

1 ☐ dies.
2 ☐ says, 'I love you' to Miranda.
3 ☐ meets his father in the forest.

b Prospero . . .

1 ☐ says, 'Kill my brother' to Ariel.
2 ☐ is angry because Miranda loves Ferdinand.
3 ☐ is happy because Ferdinand loves Miranda.

c Ariel . . .

1 ☐ plays his magic music to Caliban.
2 ☐ says, 'Your brother wants to kill you' to Alonso.
3 ☐ takes Gonzalo to Prospero.

5 Lovers & Fools

Ferdinand carries wood into Prospero's **cave**, and Miranda watches him.
'Stop working,' she says, 'and sit down for a minute.'

Ferdinand sits down. 'What's your name?' he asks.
'Miranda,' she says. And then she remembers her father's **words**, 'Oh, no! I can't talk to him!'

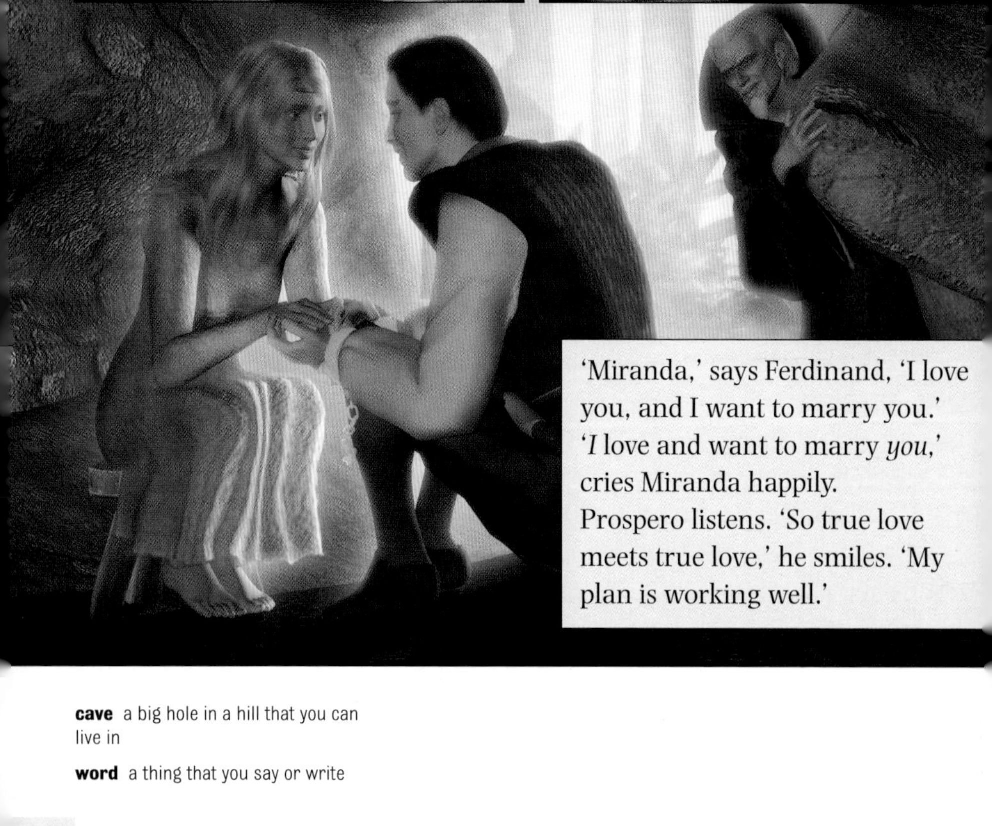

'Miranda,' says Ferdinand, 'I love you, and I want to marry you.'
'*I* love and want to marry *you*,' cries Miranda happily.
Prospero listens. 'So true love meets true love,' he smiles. 'My plan is working well.'

cave a big hole in a hill that you can live in

word a thing that you say or write

In a different part of the island, Caliban is angry. 'Here I am carrying wood for Prospero,' he says. 'Me, the true king of this island!'

'Oh no! It's one of the master's spirits, and it's coming for me. I'm sorry Prospero. Forget my bad words. Please don't attack me.'

But it's only Trinculo, the King's **fool**.

He looks at Caliban. 'What's this?' he says. 'Is it a **fish**?'
'Go away!' cries Caliban from under his **raincoat**.

It begins to rain. Trinculo gets under the raincoat with Caliban.

fool a man who works to make a king laugh

fish an animal that lives in water

raincoat a coat that you wear in the rain

Then Stephano arrives. He is King Alonso's **butler**, and Trinculo's friend. He is drinking **wine** and singing.
'Don't attack me, master,' says Caliban.
'Oh! Oh!' cries Trinculo. He is afraid too.

'Attack you?' says Stephano. 'You strange monster with two heads! Of course not!' And he gives Caliban some wine.
Under the raincoat Trinculo listens carefully. 'Is that you, Stephano?' he asks.

Trinculo comes out from under the raincoat. 'Oh, I'm happy to see you!' he says to Stephano.
'And *I'm* happy to see *you*!' says Stephano.
Caliban watches them. He is **surprised**.

'Come with me!' says Caliban. 'I can show you everything on this island!'
Trinculo and Stephano follow him.

butler a man who brings food and drink to an important person

wine a red or white drink; when you drink a lot you feel happy and sleepy

surprised suddenly feeling that something very new is happening

After some time they sit down.
'Give me more wine!' says Caliban.
'Here you are, you strange fishy monster!' says Stephano.
Caliban drinks. 'You can be the king of this island,' he says.

'King of this island?' says Stephano, surprised. 'How?'
'Prospero is the king now, but I hate him!' says Caliban. 'Go on! Kill him when he's sleeping and **throw** his magic book in the fire. Then you can be the king.'

Suddenly they hear Ariel's strange music, but they can't see him.
'Don't be afraid!' says Caliban. 'There's strange music all over the island.'

'I'm not afraid,' says Trinculo. 'Let's follow that music now, and kill Prospero later!'
So Caliban, Trinculo, and Stephano follow the music.

hrow to make something move from our hand through the air

READING CHECK

Correct seven more mistakes.

Ferdinand carries ~~water~~ wood for Prospero, and Miranda watches him. Then Miranda and Ferdinand stand and talk. Ferdinand wants to attack Miranda, and Miranda wants to kill Ferdinand. Prospero listens and isn't happy.

In a different part of the island Caliban finds breakfast for Prospero. It stops raining. Trinculo and Stephano find Caliban. Caliban wants them to kill Ariel. In the end, they don't kill him, but they follow Ariel's music.

WORD WORK

1 **Find eight more words from Chapter 5 in Prospero's magic fire.**

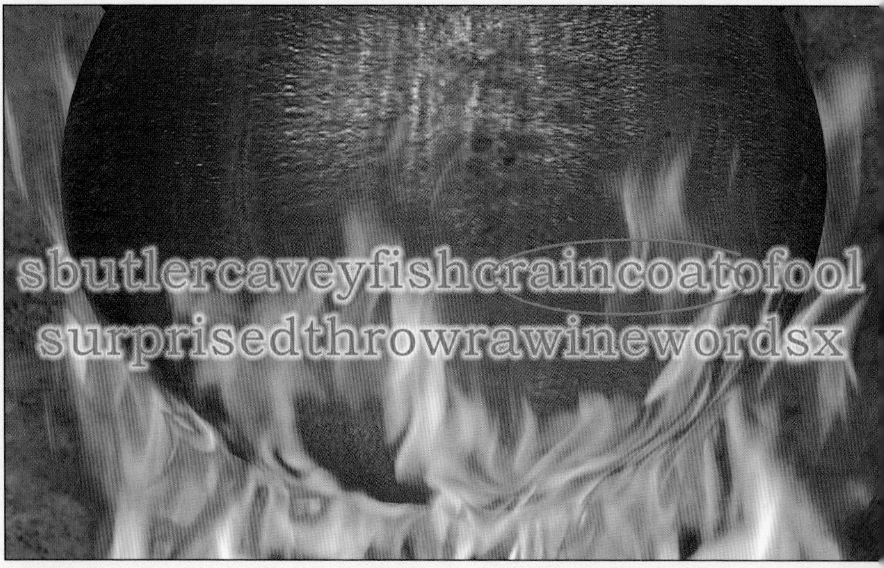

Use the words from Activity 1 to complete these sentences.

a Caliban is wearing a big ..raincoat..

b Trinculo looks at Caliban. 'It's a .... !' he thinks.

c Trinculo works for Alonso. He is the king's ....

d Stephano works for Alonso. He is the king's ....

e Stephano is drinking from a bottle of ....

f Caliban tells Stephano, '.................. Prospero's magic book in the fire!'

g Caliban is .... because Trinculo and Stephano are friends. 'They're people – not bad spirits,' he thinks.

h Prospero lives in a ....

i Caliban often says bad .... about Prospero.

There are seven more letters in the fire. Write them in order and find the name of Caliban's dead mother.

S _ _ _ _ _ _

GUESS WHAT

What happens in the next chapter? Match the two parts of the sentences.

a Alonso is happy to . . .	**1** be king of the island again.
b Caliban can. . .	**2** feel bad and go back to the ship.
c Ariel needs to . . .	**3** see Ferdinand with Miranda.
d Stephano and Trinculo . . .	**4** help Prospero one last time.
e Miranda and Ferdinand want to . . .	**5** leave the island and go back to Milan.
f Prospero wants to . . .	**6** marry in Naples.

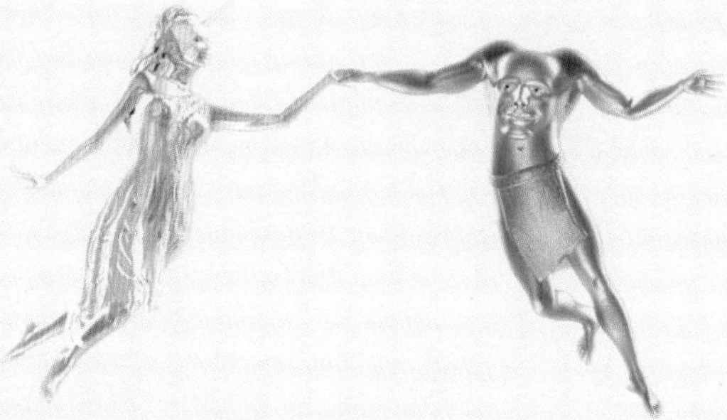

6 Happy Endings

'I'm sorry to **treat** you badly,' Prospero tells Ferdinand. 'You and my daughter want to marry, I know. And I'm happy for the two of you. Look after her, Ferdinand.'

'And now the goddesses of the island are here to sing for you on this happy day,' smiles Prospero. The goddesses Iris, Juno, and Ceres sing, and the island spirits **dance**. Everyone feels happy.

Suddenly Ariel arrives and speaks quietly in Prospero's ear. 'Caliban, Stephano, and Trinculo are coming to kill you,' he says.

treat to do something to someone with good or bad feelings

dance to move beautifully to music

Prospero stops the singing and dancing, and Ferdinand and Miranda go into the cave.

Then Prospero gives Ariel some expensive **clothes**. 'Put these in front of Caliban, Stephano, and Trinculo,' he says. Ariel takes them away.

When Stephano and Trinculo see the clothes, they stop thinking about Prospero.
'This is a beautiful coat for a king,' says Stephano.
'Very nice,' says Trinculo.
'Leave those clothes!' cries Caliban. 'We must kill Prospero first!'

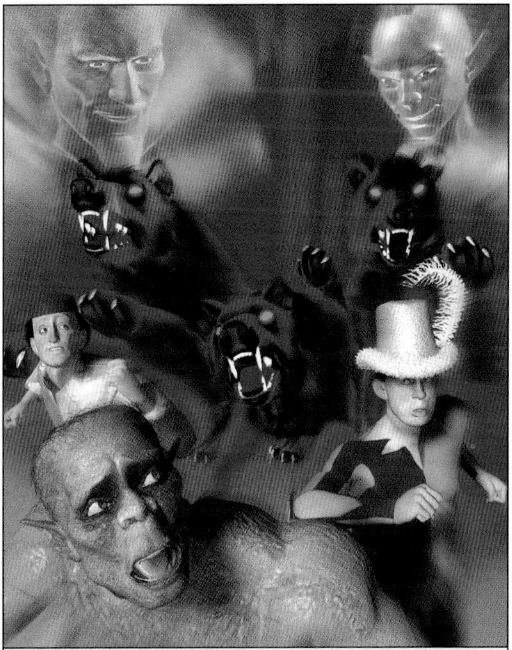

Prospero calls some spirit dogs. The dogs attack Stephano, Trinculo, and Caliban, and they run away, afraid.

clothes things that you wear

By magic Antonio, Alonso, Sebastian, and Gonzalo arrive in front of Prospero.
'Well, how shall I treat these prisoners?' Prospero asks Ariel. 'Are they sorry for their past crimes?'
'Yes, they are,' says Ariel.

'Now get my Duke's clothes,' he tells Ariel. 'And bring their ship here. Soon you can be **free**.'
'Yes, master,' says Ariel.

Prospero's prisoners wake up.
'Prospero!' they cry. They are very surprised when they see him.
'Thank you for helping me in Milan, Gonzalo,' smiles Prospero.
Then he turns to Antonio and Sebastian. 'I know your bad **hearts**,' he says darkly. 'Now, Antonio, my brother, you must give Milan back to me. You're not the Duke of Milan, you know.'

'Ah, Prospero. My son is dead,' cries Alonso. 'And my daughter is **lost** too,' says Prospero.

free with no master

heart the centre of feeling in somebody

lost that you cannot find

break to make one thing into many little parts

agree to say 'yes'

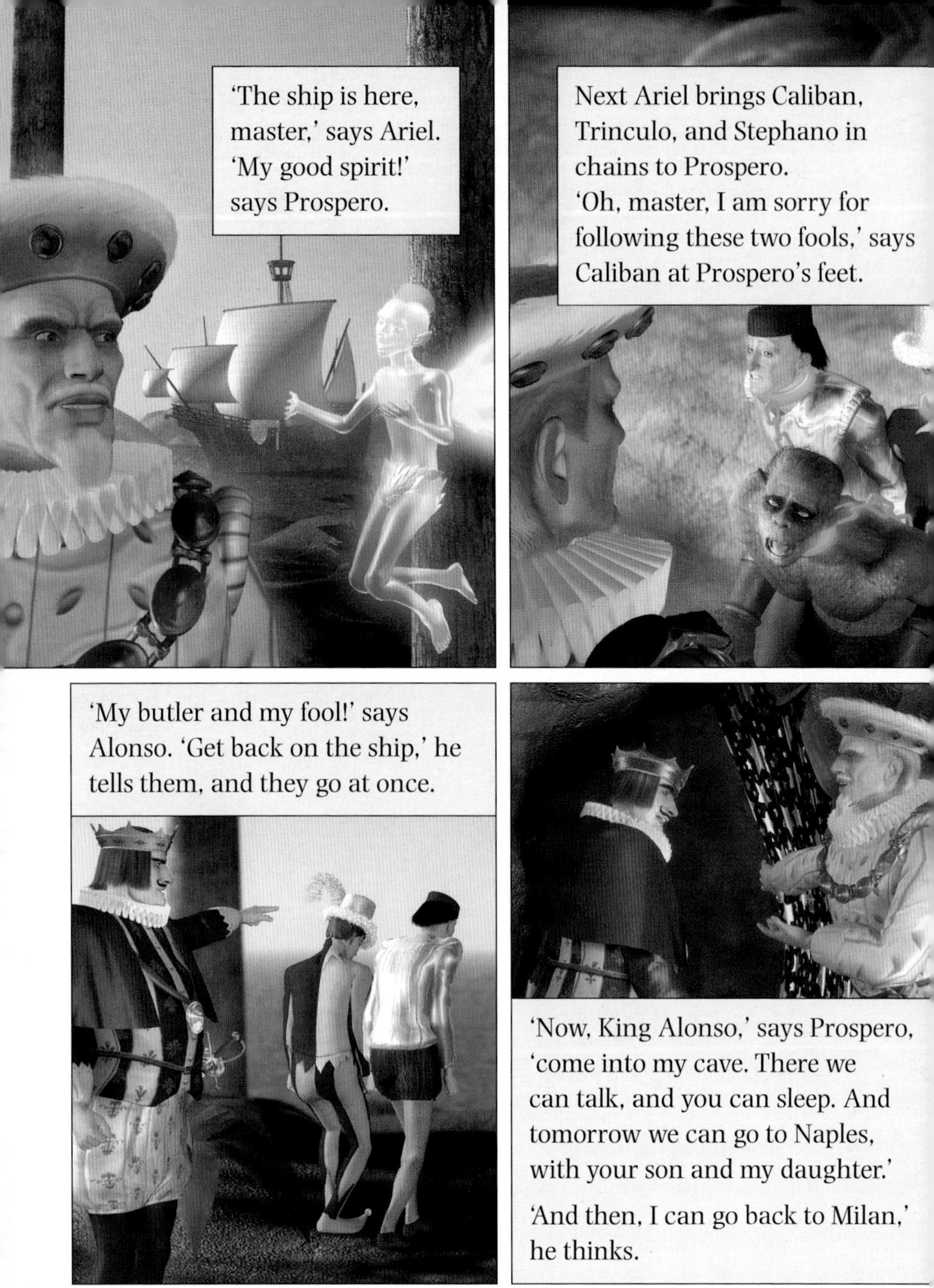
'The ship is here, master,' says Ariel. 'My good spirit!' says Prospero.
Next Ariel brings Caliban, Trinculo, and Stephano in chains to Prospero. 'Oh, master, I am sorry for following these two fools,' says Caliban at Prospero's feet.
'My butler and my fool!' says Alonso. 'Get back on the ship,' he tells them, and they go at once.
'Now, King Alonso,' says Prospero, 'come into my cave. There we can talk, and you can sleep. And tomorrow we can go to Naples, with your son and my daughter.'
'And then, I can go back to Milan,' he thinks.

tick a long thin piece of wood

READING CHECK

Put the sentences in the correct order. Number them 1–8.

- **a** ☐ Prospero attacks Stephano, Trinculo, and Caliban with spirit dogs.
- **b** [1] Iris, Juno, and Ceres sing for Ferdinand and Miranda.
- **c** ☐ Ariel brings King Alonso's ship near to Prospero's cave.
- **d** ☐ Alonso is happy when he sees Ferdinand with Miranda.
- **e** ☐ Prospero calls Antonio, Alonso, Sebastian, and Gonzalo to him.
- **f** ☐ Prospero says goodbye to Ariel and his magic book.
- **g** ☐ Ariel brings Caliban, Trinculo, and Stephano in chains to Prospero.
- **h** ☐ Stephano, Trinculo, and Caliban come to kill Prospero.

WORD WORK

Find words in the puzzle to complete the sentences on page 39.

a There is lots of singing and ..dancing.. when Ferdinand and Miranda say, 'We want to marry!'

b Prospero .... Gonzalo nicely.

c Prospero puts on his old .... from Milan so Antonio, Alonso, Sebastian, and Gonzalo know him.

d Prospero tells Alonso, 'My daughter is ....!'

e 'Ferdinand and Miranda are dead,' thinks Alonso, and he tells Prospero, 'My .... is ....!'

f Alonso .... with Ferdinand's plan to marry Miranda.

g Prospero breaks his magic ....

h In the end Ariel is ....

GUESS WHAT

What happens after the story ends? Choose from these ideas or add your own.

a ☐ Caliban is king of the island.

b ☐ A girl monster – 'Calibana' – arrives on the island.

c ☐ Caliban finds Prospero's book, and learns magic.

d ☐ The island spirits are nice to him now.

e ☐ Caliban and Calibana have lots of little baby 'Calibans'.

f ☐ Ferdinand is the Duke of Milan when Prospero dies.

g ☐ Ariel feels alone and comes to Milan.

h ☐ ....

i ☐ ....

j ☐ ....

Project A *Living on a desert island*

1 What does Prospero do on his desert island? Look at the pictures below and complete the poster. Use a dictionary to help you.

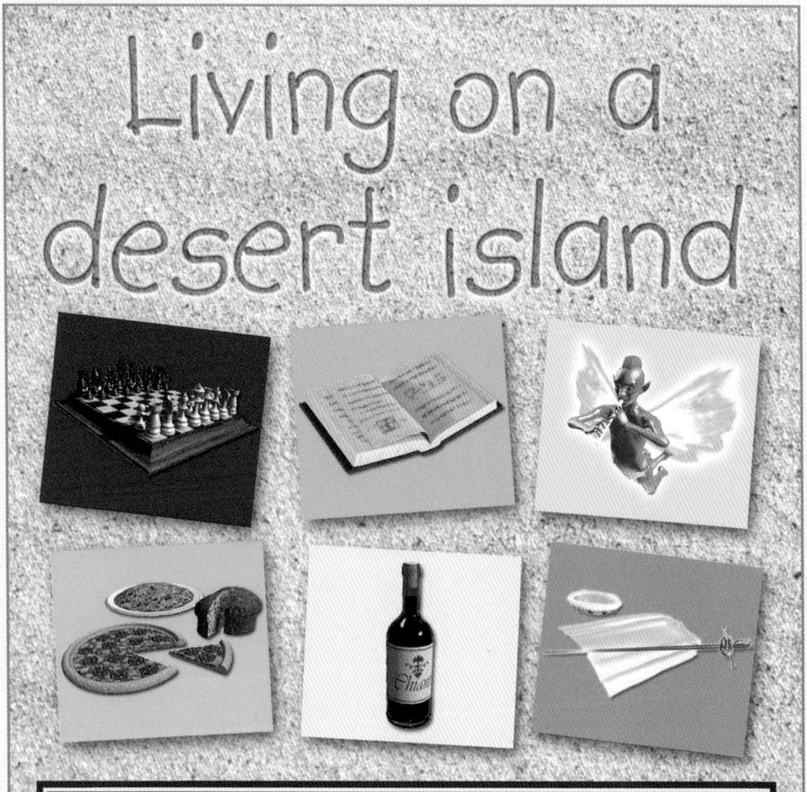

1 I listen to the spirit ....'s music.

2 I eat good Italian ....

3 I read my .... book.

4 I drink good Italian ....

5 I play .... with Miranda.

6 Sometimes I wear my .... and my Duke's ....

PROJECTS

You are going to a desert island. What do you want to take with you? Write six things.

a some music to listen to ....

b something to eat ....

c something to read ....

d something to drink ....

e something to play with ....

f something to wear ....

What do you do with your things on the desert island? Make a poster.

Living on a desert island

1 ....

2 ....

3 ....

4 ....

5 ....

6 ....

Project B *A letter in a bottle*

1 This is a letter in a bottle from one of the people in the story. The letter is asking for help. Who is it from?

GONZALO

PROSPERO

STEPHANO

Dear Friend,

Help! Here we are on a magic island – between North Africa and Naples – after a terrible storm. Our ship is lost. I am here with my master the King of Naples, his brother, and the Duke of Milan. Prince Ferdinand is lost too, and we must find him. The island is very green. There are lots of spirits here, things to eat on magic tables, and strange music in the air.

Please bring your ship here at once, and come and find us . . .

PROJECTS

Complete this letter in a bottle from Trinculo.

Dear Friend,

Help! Here we are on a magic island – between North Africa and Naples – after a terrible storm. Our ship is lost.

I am here with my friend .... He is the King of Naples' .... I am the King of Naples' .... The King's name is .... Here on the island there is a strange monster. His name is .... He has a master too. His name is .... There are magic .... to wear, and sometimes magic .... run after you.

Please bring your ship here at once, and come and find us.

Trinculo

3 Now complete this letter in a bottle from Ferdinand.

....

Help! Here .... – between North Africa and Naples – .... storm. Our .... I am here alone. I can't find my father, the .... , or his men.

Here on the island .... His name is .... He has .... Her .... Miranda. I .... her.

Please ....

....

4 You are lost on a magic island. Write your letter in a bottle.

Dear Friend,

GRAMMAR CHECK

Countable and uncountable nouns

Nouns can be countable or uncountable. Countable nouns can be singular or plural, uncountable nouns have only one form.

We use an before singular countable nouns that start with a vowel sound.

an angry father *an important plan* *an old word*

We use a/an for a thing in general. We use the for a specific thing.

Singular countable nouns	Plural countable nouns
a gate, the gate	*gates, the gates, some gates*
an island, the island	*islands, the islands, some islands*

We don't use a/an + uncountable noun.

water – the water – some water ✓ *a water* ✗

music – *the music – some music* ✓ *a music* ✗

Complete the sentences with *a/an* or *some*.

a In the boat Prospero finds ...a... letter, ...some... clothes, and ...some... water.

b On the island there are .... spirits and .... strange monster.

c 'Bring us .... wood for .... fire,' Prospero tells Caliban.

d Ferdinand hears .... music and sees .... beautiful woman.

e 'You aren't .... important king or .... prince, you're .... spy.'

f They hear .... strange noise and .... beautiful music.

g They see .... magic table with .... wine, and .... things to eat on it.

h Ariel takes them .... clothes. Stephano puts on .... expensive coat and Trinculo takes .... hat.

Complete the sentences with *a/an* or *the*.

a Antonio's ...the... new Duke of Milan.

b Alonso's .... King of Naples.

c Gonzalo's .... old man.

d Trinculo's .... fool.

e Ferdinand's .... Prince of Naples.

f Juno's .... goddess.

GRAMMAR CHECK

Countable and uncountable nouns: some and any

We use some in positive sentences and when we offer things or make requests.

Some women look after Miranda. *Can you bring me some wood?*

Would you like some wine?

We use any in negative sentences and in most questions.

Caliban hasn't got any friends. *Are there any men on the ship?*

Can you hear any strange noises?

3 Complete the sentences. Use *some* or *any* and one of the words in the box.

chains	~~clothes~~	friends	men	music
noises	people	spirits	wine	women

a Gonzalo puts some clothes in the boat for Prospero and Miranda.

b There aren't .... on the island when Prospero and Miranda arrive.

c There are .... on the ship but there aren't ....

d 'I can't hear .... strange ....,' says Alonso.

e Ferdinand hears .... beautiful .... He doesn't see ....

f 'Can you bring me .... for this spy?' Prospero asks Ariel.

g 'Have you got .... here?' Miranda asks Ferdinand.

h 'Would you like to drink .... ?' Prospero asks Alonso.

4 Rewrite these sentences about the story to make them true.

a There aren't any spirits on the island.

There are some spirits on the island.

b Caliban has got some friends on the island.

....

c Prospero can't see any people on the ship by magic.

....

d The storm kills some of the people on the ship.

....

e Sebastian and Antonio don't hear any strange noises on the island.

....

GRAMMAR

GRAMMAR CHECK

Comparative adjectives

To make comparative forms, add –er to short adjectives.	*tall – taller*
When adjectives end in –e we add –r.	*nice – nicer*
When adjectives end in a short vowel + single consonant, we double the last consonant and add –er.	*big – bigger*
When adjectives end in consonant + –y, we change y to i and add –er.	*happy – happier*
With long adjectives we use more.	*interesting – more interesting*
Some adjectives have an irregular comparative form.	*good – better* *bad – worse*
Use than after comparative adjectives.	*My magic is stronger than your sword.*

Write the comparatives.

a strange stranger
d fat ....
g new ....
b difficult ....
e hungry ....
h expensive ....
c angry ....
f careful ....
i early ....

Write comparative sentences about Ariel and Caliban.

a friendly Ariel's friendlier than Caliban.
b angry ....
c beautiful ....
d big ....
e strong ....
f difficult ....
g little ....
h nice ....

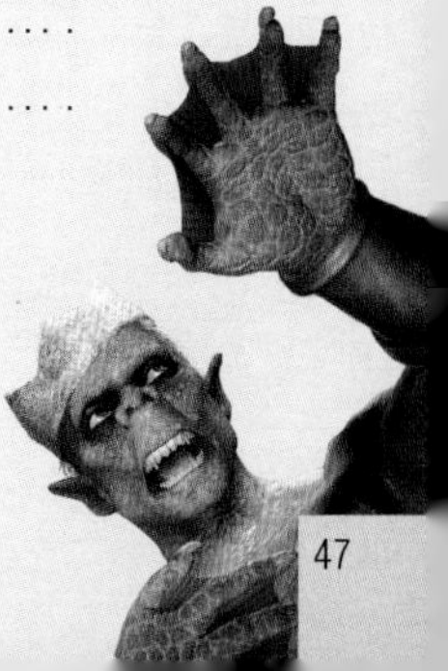

GRAMMAR CHECK

Modal auxiliary verbs: can and can't

We use can/can't + infinitive without *to* to talk about things we know how (or don't know how) to do, and things it is possible (or not possible) for us to do.

Ferdinand can hear Ariel but he can't see him.

Can Prospero do magic? *Yes, he can.*

We use Can …? when we make requests or ask for permission.

Can you make a magic storm? *Can I marry Ferdinand?*

7 Write questions and answers about the story.

- **a** Miranda / do magic Can Miranda do magic? No, she can't.
- **b** Caliban / speak ……………………………………? ……………………
- **c** Ariel / fly ……………………………………? ……………………
- **d** Ferdinand / swim ……………………………………? ……………………
- **e** Caliban / play music ……………………………………? ……………………
- **f** King Alonso / see Ariel ……………………………………? ……………………
- **g** King Alonso / hear Ariel ……………………………………? ……………………
- **h** Miranda / marry Ferdinand ……………………………………? ……………………

8 What do these people say in these situations? Use *Can you …?* or *Can I …?* and th words in brackets.

- **a** Prospero wants to see the island. He says to Caliban:
  (show) 'Can you show me the island?'
- **b** Prospero wants Miranda to see Ferdinand. He says to Ariel:
  (bring / here) '……………………………………?'
- **c** Miranda wants to speak to Ferdinand. She says to Prospero:
  (speak) '……………………………………?'
- **d** Antonio wants to kill Alonso and Gonzalo. He says to Sebastian:
  (kill) '……………………………………?'
- **e** Caliban likes wine. He says to Trinculo:
  (have) '……………………………………?'
- **f** Ferdinand wants to marry Miranda. He says to Prospero:
  (daughter) '……………………………………?'

GRAMMAR CHECK

Adverbs of manner

We use adverbs of manner to describe actions. They tell us more about verbs.

Miranda speaks to the prince quietly.

We make adverbs from adjectives by adding –ly.

quiet – quietly

For adjectives ending in –y, we change y to i and add –ly.

angry – angrily

Some adverbs are irregular.

fast – fast *good – well*

Circle the adverbs of manner in Ferdinand's letter.

I'm a prisoner here on a magic island. But I stay here happily. I love a beautiful woman. Her name's Miranda. Her father, Prospero, always speaks angrily to me, but she speaks to me nicely. She looks after me well when her father isn't here. She speaks quietly and watches the cave door carefully. Sometimes she looks at me strangely and she loves me, I think. What do you think? Am I right?

Choose the correct word for each sentence.

a When Caliban attacks Miranda, Prospero speaks … to him.

☐ angry ☑ angrily

b Caliban works … , but he does things when Prospero tells him.

☐ slowly ☐ careful

c Ferdinand jumps into the sea and swims away … .

☐ quietly ☐ fast

d The men sit down … at the magic table.

☐ hungrily ☐ hungry

e Before they can eat, Ariel takes the food away … .

☐ quickly ☐ strange

GRAMMAR CHECK

Present Continuous: affirmative and negative

We use the Present Continuous to talk about things that are (or are not) happening now.

People are dying in the cold sea. *My plan isn't working well.*

We don't usually use the Present Continuous with verbs of state, feelings and senses, like love, like, have, want, be, see, hear, and understand.

I understand. ✓	*I am understanding.* ✗
I don't understand. ✓	*I am not understanding.* ✗
I love you. ✓	*I am loving you.* ✗
I don't love you. ✓	*I am not loving you.* ✗

11 Complete the text about the picture with the verbs in the correct form.

Prospero a) is standing (stand) in the door of his cave. He b) .... (have) the magic book in his hands. He c) .... (look) angrily at the book and he d) .... (call) Ariel. Prospero e) .... (want) Ariel to find his brother. Miranda and Ferdinand f) .... (stand) behind Prospero. They g) .... (talk) quietly. Miranda's hand h) .... (be) on Ferdinand's arm. She i) .... (not / understand) her father. Miranda j) .... (wear) a white dress and she k) .... (look) very beautiful.

12 Write about the picture. Use these words: *be, talk, want, do something bad, sleep on the ground, sit down, wear,* and *red hat*.

The four men are on the island.

....

....

....

GRAMMAR CHECK

Making offers and suggestions with shall and let's

When we make suggestions we can use Shall I …? Shall we …? **or** Let's … **+ infinitive without** *to*.

Shall I kill Alonso *for you?* *Shall we follow* the music? *Let's look for* Ferdinand.

We can also use Shall I/We **in Wh- questions to ask for suggestions.**

What shall I do with these prisoners?

We can make offers with Shall I …? **+ infinitive with** *to*.

'Shall I show you the island?'

Write suggestions with *Shall I …?*, *Shall we …?*, or *Let's …* + infinitive without *to* using words from each box.

follow	get	attack	make	put on	~~show~~	stay

~~the island~~	the music	on the ship	the ship
some food	a fire	these clothes	

a Prospero and Miranda are new on the island. Caliban asks them:
'......Shall I show you the island......?'

b It is very cold in the cave. Caliban asks Prospero:
'..?'

c Ferdinand looks hungry. Miranda asks him:
'..?'

d 'There's a ship near my island.' Prospero tells Ariel:
'..'

e The ship is going down in the storm. Antonio asks his friends:
'..?'

f Ferdinand wakes up and hears music. He asks himself:
'..?'

g The three fools see some beautiful new clothes. Trinculo asks Stephano:
'..?'

DOMINOES Your Choice

Read *Dominoes* for pleasure, or to develop language skills. It's your choice.

Each *Domino* reader includes:
- a good story to enjoy
- integrated activities to develop reading skills and increase vocabulary
- task-based projects – perfect for CEFR portfolios
- contextualized grammar activities

Each *Domino* pack contains a reader, and an excitingly dramatized audio recording of the story

If you liked this *Domino*, read these:

The Happy Prince

Oscar Wilde

The Happy Prince is a beautiful golden statue high up on a column in the city. Everyone loves him.

He feels sad about the city's poor people, but what can he do? He can't leave his column. Then the swallow arrives, and helps the Happy Prince to do many good things.

But what about the swallow's dream of flying to Egypt? And what does the Mayor do when the Happy Prince loses all his gold?

Mulan

Retold by Janet Hardy-Gould

When the Emperor calls every man to join the army and fight the enemy, Mulan's father is old and ill, and cannot go. Wearing men's clothes and riding a horse, Mulan leaves her family and fights bravely for the Emperor in her father's place.

She is soon a hero for all the soldiers in the Chinese army. One of them, Ye Ming, is her best friend. But does he know that she is a woman? And can Mulan fall in love with a friend?

	CEFR	Cambridge Exams	IELTS	TOEFL iBT	TOEIC
Level 3	B1	PET	4.0	57-86	550
Level 2	A2–B1	KET-PET	3.0-4.0	–	390
Level 1	A1–A2	YLE Flyers/KET	3.0	–	225
Starter & Quick Starter	A1	YLE Movers	1.0–2.0	–	–

You can find details and a full list of books and teachers' resources on our website: www.oup.com/elt/gradedreaders